Hostile Hallways:

The AAUW Survey on
Sexual Harassment in America's Schools

Commissioned by

The American Association of University Women
Educational Foundation

Researched by

Harris/Scholastic Research
a division of Louis Harris and Associates, Inc.
in partnership with Scholastic, Inc.
Study number: 923012

WHY A SURVEY ON SEXUAL HARASSMENT?

With the publication of *Hostile Hallways: The AAUW Survey on Sexual Harassment in America's Schools,* the AAUW Educational Foundation has taken another significant step toward our goal: a school climate that is equitable for all students—an environment in which all girls and boys can flourish. The Foundation undertook this research—the first nationally representative survey of adolescent sexual harassment in school—to increase understanding and awareness of this very complex problem.

While much is known about sexual harassment in the workplace, very little is known about sexual harassment in school. We believe the startling information presented here will help everyone concerned with our children's education to begin to foster a fairer and healthier school environment.

In the late 1980s, the AAUW Educational Foundation broadened its mission—we expanded it to include the equitable education of girls. Until that time, AAUW Foundation efforts centered on awarding post-graduate fellowships to women, a group shamefully underrepresented in many areas of higher education. In 1988, the Board of Directors voted to respond to disturbing research that showed that girls were not being adequately prepared for the future. Although equity in education had been mandated by federal law in 1972, studies continued to indicate that girls were not receiving the same quality of education as boys.

The AAUW Educational Foundation established a new research program to provide the information needed to help girls become better educated and more self-assured women. In 1991, AAUW released its ground-breaking *Shortchanging Girls, Shortchanging America*, a nationwide poll that assessed the attitudes, educational experiences, math and science interest, and career aspirations of girls and boys ages 9 to 15. The most interesting and troubling findings centered on self-esteem. As boys and girls grow up, both experience a loss of self-esteem in a variety of areas. However, the loss is most dramatic—and has the greatest, longest-lasting impact—for girls.

Following *Shortchanging Girls, Shortchanging America*, the AAUW Educational Foundation in 1992 released *The AAUW Report: How Schools Shortchange Girls*, a synthesis of all the available research on the subject of girls in school. The report revealed alarming and pervasive patterns of gender bias and inequity. It highlighted a problem of national proportions and shattered the common assumption that girls and boys are treated equally in our public schools. Also uncovered in the course of this research: a hostile environment in America's schools—sexual harassment was on the rise.

This finding prompted the AAUW Educational Foundation to underwrite this in-depth survey of girls, boys, and sexual harassment in public schools. With funds raised by AAUW members and other supporters, the Foundation commissioned Louis Harris and Associates to survey more than 1,600 public school students—female and male; African American, white, and Hispanic—in grades 8 through 11.

The questions we wanted answered: How widespread is sexual harassment in school? Who is doing it. . .and to whom? Where is it happening? What forms does it take? How are kids affected by it—what happens to their attitudes toward school and their ability to learn, grow, and achieve?

The findings presented here confirm that sexual harassment is a major problem for many students. Not unlike their adult counterparts in the workplace, children in school are experiencing unwanted advances. Students, however, are required by law to remain in school and thus have the right to be safe there. Beyond a doubt, we now know that sexual harassment in the classrooms and hallways of America's schools is a major problem—one we can no longer afford to ignore. Unchecked, it will continue to deny millions of children the educational environment they need to grow into healthy, educated adults. All of us have a responsibility for the educational experiences of America's children: all of us must now accept that responsibility and begin to create—and maintain—schools that are free of sexual harassment.

Alice McKee
President, 1989–1993
AAUW Educational Foundation

The startling findings on sexual harassment in *The AAUW Report: How Schools Shortchange Girls* compelled the AAUW Educational Foundation to undertake further research. We wanted to assess the extent of sexual harassment in America's schools and, even more important, the effects of that harassment on our children.

AAUW commissioned one of this country's most respected survey research firms, Louis Harris and Associates, to ensure that the survey's methodology, implementation, and questionnaire would meet the highest standards of the survey research community. The survey was designed to provide a profile of the problem of sexual harassment in school and answer many of the questions about school-based sexual harassment. In addition to measuring the extent of sexual harassment in school, AAUW was determined to identify the educational, emotional, and behavioral impact of sexual harassment on our nation's schoolchildren.

The results of this survey form a bleak picture: 4 out of 5 students have experienced some form of sexual harassment in school. And while the impact of sexual harassment in school is significant for all students, girls suffer greater effects than boys. Further, the level of sexual harassment of boys is surprisingly high.

For many, the analysis that follows will confirm their worst fears about sexual harassment in school; for others, the results will be surprising and shocking.

What will be clear to all is that sexual harassment in America's schools affects—even disables—girls and boys alike.

What remains is the challenge facing students, teachers, and parents to ensure that the behaviors detailed in this survey do not continue.

THE SURVEY

Methodology

The survey was conducted in February and March 1993. A total of 1,632 field surveys was completed by public school students in grades 8 through 11, from 79 schools across the continental United States. While further study of other groups is needed, the scope of this study contains representative samples for Hispanic, white, and African American students. These samples are large enough to analyze with confidence the specific experiences, behaviors, and attitudes of these groups by gender. The national probability sample of schools and students is based on a highly stratified two-stage sampling design. The findings are projectable to all public school students in the 8th through 11th grades in the United States. At a 95% confidence level, the margin of error is plus or minus 4 percentage points. Among smaller subgroups, the margin of error may be greater, but not significantly so.

Implementation

Letters were mailed to the principals of randomly selected schools, requesting their participation in the survey. The Harris firm then contacted the principals by telephone to confirm their willingness to participate. Classes and grades were randomly selected within schools.

Professionally trained Harris facilitators administered the surveys in each of the participating 79 classes, requesting that the teacher of each class sampled remain outside the classroom while the students filled out the surveys. Those teachers who wanted to remain were asked to stay in the front of the classroom.

To further reassure the students of the anonymity of their responses, they were asked to put their completed surveys into envelopes and seal them. The surveys were then given to the Harris facilitator and sent immediately to the Harris firm for tabulation.

Each participating school was given a credit

STUDENTS WERE ASKED...

During your whole school life, how often, if at all, has anyone
(this includes students, teachers, other school employees, or anyone else)
done the following things to you <u>when you did not want them to</u>?

- Made sexual comments, jokes, gestures, or looks.
- Showed, gave, or left you sexual pictures, photographs, illustrations, messages, or notes.
- Wrote sexual messages/graffiti about you on bathroom walls, in locker rooms, etc.
- Spread sexual rumors about you.
- Said you were gay or lesbian.
- Spied on you as you dressed or showered at school.
- Flashed or "mooned" you.

- Touched, grabbed, or pinched you in a sexual way.
- Pulled at your clothing in a sexual way.
- Intentionally brushed against you in a sexual way.
- Pulled your clothing off or down.
- Blocked your way or cornered you in a sexual way.
- Forced you to kiss him/her.
- Forced you to do something sexual, other than kissing.

for school supplies from Scholastic, Inc., as well as a list of books, articles, and other resources on sexual harassment compiled by the AAUW Educational Foundation.

The Questionnaire

At the outset—and throughout the questionnaire—students were instructed to answer only about their **school-related experiences during school-related times**, such as: on the way to and from school, in classrooms and hallways, on school grounds during the day and after school, and on school trips. Students were asked to respond to a series of questions and to give written comments on how they felt as a result of the sexual harassment they had experienced. These comments are highlighted throughout this report.

A list of 14 types of harassment—half involving physical contact and half involving no physical contact—was pre-

Sexual harassment is unwanted and unwelcome sexual behavior which interferes with your life.

■

sented (see page 5). Experts in the field of sexual harassment who served as project advisors on this survey worked with the AAUW Educational Foundation and Harris/Scholastic to develop this list.

Students were provided with the following definition: **Sexual harassment is <u>unwanted</u> and <u>unwelcome</u> sexual behavior which interferes with your life. Sexual harassment is not behaviors that you <u>like</u> or <u>want</u> (for example: wanted kissing, touching, or flirting).**

Regarding the 14 forms of sexual harassment, students were asked to respond to the following question: "During your whole school life, how often, if at all, has anyone (this includes students, teachers, other school employees, and anyone else) done the following things to you <u>when you did not want them to?</u> Students were presented with the following choices: often, occasionally, rarely, never, and not sure.

THE PROBLEM

Sexual harassment in school is an experience common to the vast majority of 8th-to-11th-grade students in America's public schools. Clearly the most alarming finding of this survey is that fully 4 out of 5 students (81%) report that they have been the target of some form of sexual harassment during their school lives.

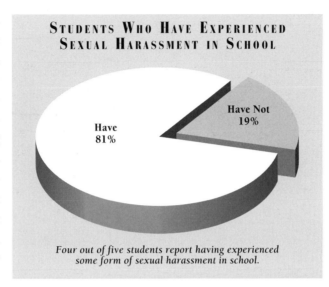

STUDENTS WHO HAVE EXPERIENCED SEXUAL HARASSMENT IN SCHOOL

Four out of five students report having experienced some form of sexual harassment in school.

are more likely to have experienced sexual harassment than whites (75%) and Hispanics (69%). For all the girls surveyed: 87% of whites report having experienced sexual harassment, compared with 84% of African Americans and 82% of Hispanics.

Who is being harassed?

Among the 81% who report being harassed, the gender gap is surprisingly narrow: 85% of girls and 76% of boys surveyed say they have experienced unwanted and unwelcome sexual behavior that interferes with their lives. The gap widens, however, when we look at frequency. If we consider the statistics for the 58% of students who report experiencing at least one form of harassment "often" or "occasionally," we see a 17-point gender gap: 66% of girls and 49% of boys. Of those experiencing harassment, 1 in 4 report being targeted "often." The percentage of girls reporting this is 31, compared with 18% of the boys.

In the racial breakdowns of sexual harassment in school there are greater gaps among boys than there are among girls. For all the boys surveyed: African Americans (81%)

When does sexual harassment start?

A student's first experience of sexual harassment is most likely to occur in the middle school/junior high years of 6th to 9th grade: 47% of the students who have been harassed fall into this group—40% of boys and 54% of girls. One-third of those students (32%) who have been harassed first experience such unwelcome behavior before 7th grade. For girls, the percentage is 34; for boys, 32. Four in 10 African American girls (42%) and Hispanic girls (40%) have been targeted this early, compared with 31% of white girls. Some students (6%) first experienced unwanted advances before the 3rd grade—notably 10% of Hispanic girls.

Twice as many boys (36%) as girls (18%) who have been harassed are unable to recall the grade in which they first experienced unwelcome sexual behavior in school.

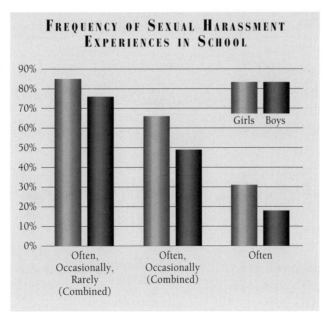

FREQUENCY OF SEXUAL HARASSMENT EXPERIENCES IN SCHOOL

Girls Boys

Often, Occasionally, Rarely (Combined) · Often, Occasionally (Combined) · Often

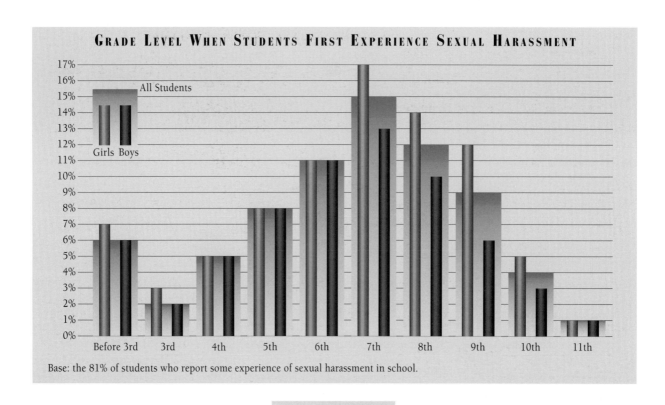

GRADE LEVEL WHEN STUDENTS FIRST EXPERIENCE SEXUAL HARASSMENT

Base: the 81% of students who report some experience of sexual harassment in school.

What forms of sexual harassment are students experiencing?

Although the lines often blur, it is generally understood that there are different types and varying degrees of sexual harassment. This survey categorized 14 forms of harassment, half physical (grabbing, pinching, forced kissing, for example) and half involving no physical contact (including making sexual comments, spreading sexual rumors, and flashing).

At one end of the spectrum, two-thirds of all students surveyed say they have been the targets of **sexual comments, jokes, gestures, or looks**—76% of girls and 56% of boys report having experienced this most common form of harassment. At the other extreme, 11% report being **forced to do something sexual other than kissing**—13% of girls and 9% of boys say they have experienced this form of unwelcome sexual behavior. In between is a variety of sexual harassment experiences, both physical and nonphysical.

"It made me feel guilty. I was upset. I was scared. I knew it was all wrong. It happened too fast. I can't sleep at night."

African American
female
age 14

The second most common form of sexual harassment involves **touching, grabbing and/or pinching in a sexual way** (53%), as reported by 65% of girls and 42% of boys—a 23-point gender gap.

Among the 46% of students who say they have been **intentionally brushed up against in a sexual way**, the gender gap is a significant 21 points: 57% of girls and 36% of boys. African American girls (64%) are more likely to have experienced this physical form of harassment than white girls (58%) and Hispanic girls (49%). Among boys, nearly half of all African Americans (49%), compared with 34% of whites and 29% of Hispanics, have been targets of this behavior.

The gender gap narrows in the case of **mooning and flashing**, with 49% of girls and 41% of boys reporting this experience. There are significant disparities along racial/ethnic lines, for both girls and boys. White girls (54%) are much more likely to have experienced this harassment than Hispanic (38%) and African Ameri-

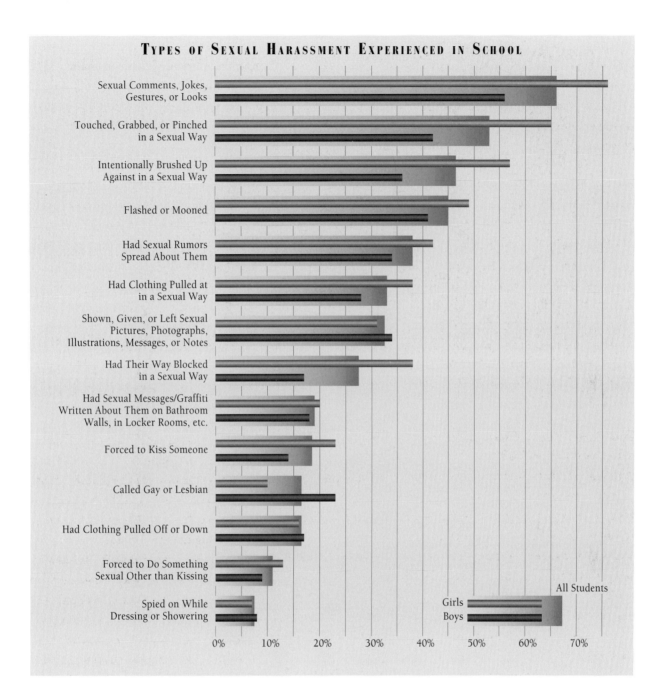

TYPES OF SEXUAL HARASSMENT EXPERIENCED IN SCHOOL

can (35%) girls. Roughly equal percentages of white boys (43%) and African American boys (41%) have been flashed or mooned when they did not want to be, compared with only 29% of Hispanic boys.

More than one-third of students (37%) have been the **target of sexual rumors**—the fifth most common form of sexual harassment in school. Among girls: 42% have been victimized this way—African Americans (49%), whites (42%), and Hispanics (33%). Among boys: 34%

have had this experience—African Americans (36%), whites (34%), and Hispanics (29%).

The sixth most common form of sexual harassment in school is **having one's clothes pulled at in a sexual way**. One-third of students have experienced this, with girls (38%) more likely than boys (28%) to have been targeted. Again, African American girls (47%) have been subject to this behavior much more often than white (37%) and Hispanic (32%) girls. A similar pattern holds true for boys: African

Americans (38%), Hispanics and whites (26% each)—a gap of 12 points.

Slightly less than one-third of students (32%) have been **shown, given, or left unwanted sexual pictures or notes**. Interestingly, boys (34%) are more likely than girls (31%) to have been targeted in this way. Hispanic boys (27%) have been subject to this less often than white (33%) and African American (34%) boys.

More than 1 in 4 students (27%) say they have been **blocked or cornered in a sexual way**, with more than twice as many girls (38%) as boys (17%) reporting this. Among girls, 48% of African Americans have experienced this, compared with 36% of both whites and Hispanics. Roughly the same relative racial/ethnic breakdowns exist for boys.

Almost 1 in 5 students (19%) say they have been the **target of written sexual messages/graffiti** on bathroom walls, lockers, etc., with boys and girls reporting virtually equal experiences.

Among the 18% of students who say they have been **forced to kiss someone** when they did not want to, there is a gender gap of 9 points: 23% of girls and 14% of boys have been subjected to this behavior. Among girls: African Americans (30%), Hispanics (27%), and whites (22%). Among boys: African Americans (22%), Hispanics (16%), and whites (12%).

Among the 17% of students who have been **called gay or lesbian** when they did not want to be, there is a pattern-breaking gender gap of 13 points: boys (23%) are more than twice as likely as girls (10%) to have

> "It made me feel confused, whether I should tell or not. I didn't know if I was overreacting since this was a teacher I trusted and looked up to."
>
> White female age 13

been targeted. While there are no significant racial/ethnic differences among boys, Hispanic girls (5%) were only half as likely to have experienced this behavior as African American (11%) and white (10%) girls.

Of the 16% of students who say they have **had their clothing pulled off or down**, the gender breakdown is nearly equal. Of all the subgroups, African American boys (23%—nearly 1 in 4) were most likely to have been targeted.

A troubling 1 in 10 students (11%) say they have been **forced to do something sexual at school other than kissing**—13% of girls and 9% of boys. Among boys, 1 in 5 African Americans (19%) report having been targeted, compared with 13% of Hispanic boys and 6% of white boys.

Lastly, 7% of students say they have **been spied on while they dressed or showered at school**, with equal percentages of girls and boys having been targeted, though 11% say they could not be sure if they had been victimized in this way.

Who are the harassers... and why do they do it?

Of the 81%* who have been targets of sexual harassment in school, 18% say they have been harassed by a school employee (such as a teacher, coach, bus driver, teacher's aide, security guard, principal, or counselor)—1 in 4 girls (25%)

> *The statistics in this survey—except where noted—refer to the 81% of students who report some experience of sexual harassment in school.*

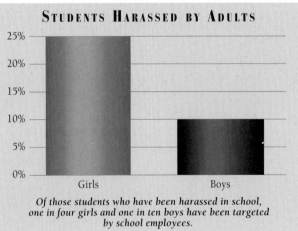

STUDENTS HARASSED BY ADULTS

Of those students who have been harassed in school, one in four girls and one in ten boys have been targeted by school employees.

and 1 in 10 boys (10%). African American girls (33%) are more likely to have been targeted by a school employee, compared with white (25%) and Hispanic (17%) girls.

But as disturbing as these numbers are, they are dwarfed by student reports of peer-to-peer harassment. Of those who say they have been harassed, nearly 4 in 5 (79%) have been targeted by a current or former student at school—86% of girls and 71% of boys. Among girls who have been harassed: 81% report having been harassed by a male acting alone, 57% by a group of males, 11% by a mixed group of males and females, 10% by a female acting alone, and 3% by a

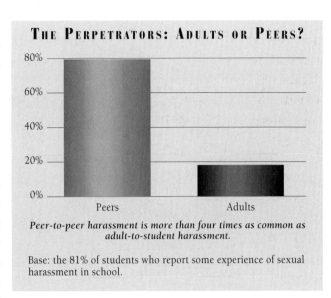

THE PERPETRATORS: ADULTS OR PEERS?

Peer-to-peer harassment is more than four times as common as adult-to-student harassment.

Base: the 81% of students who report some experience of sexual harassment in school.

group of females. Among boys who have been harassed: 57% report having been harassed by a female acting alone, 35% by a group of females, 25% by a male acting alone, 14% by a group of males, and 13% by a mixed group of females and males.

After being asked about their experiences as targets of sexual harassment, students were questioned about their experiences as perpetrators. Not surprisingly—given that nearly 4 in 5 students who have been harassed say they were targeted by a peer—we see some high numbers. Two-thirds (66%) of all boys and more than half (52%) of all girls surveyed admit they have sexually harassed someone in the

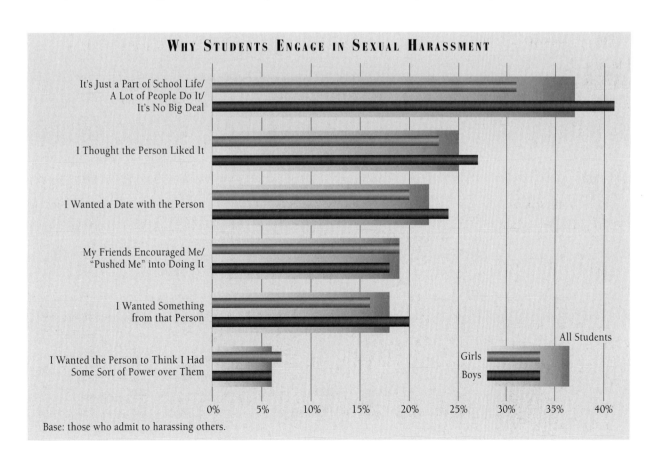

WHY STUDENTS ENGAGE IN SEXUAL HARASSMENT

Base: those who admit to harassing others.

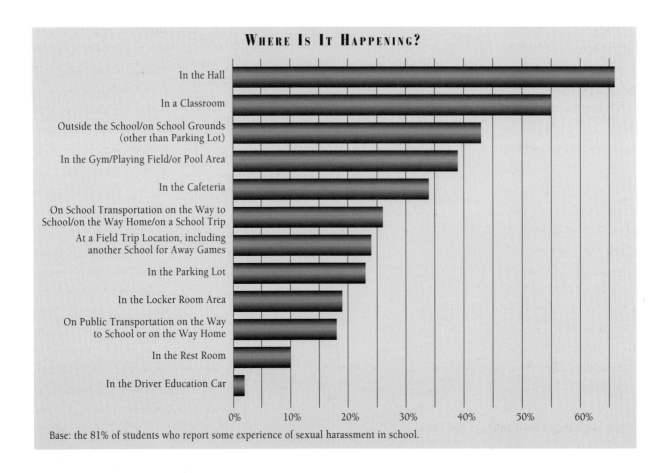

WHERE IS IT HAPPENING?

- In the Hall
- In a Classroom
- Outside the School/on School Grounds (other than Parking Lot)
- In the Gym/Playing Field/or Pool Area
- In the Cafeteria
- On School Transportation on the Way to School/on the Way Home/on a School Trip
- At a Field Trip Location, including another School for Away Games
- In the Parking Lot
- In the Locker Room Area
- On Public Transportation on the Way to School or on the Way Home
- In the Rest Room
- In the Driver Education Car

0%   10%   20%   30%   40%   50%   60%

Base: the 81% of students who report some experience of sexual harassment in school.

school setting (only 4% of these boys and girls say they harassed an adult). Among girls who have been the perpetrators of harassment, the racial/ethnic breakdown is: African Americans (63%), Hispanics and whites (50% each). Among boys, roughly equal percentages of African Americans (67%) and whites (66%) admit having engaged in such behavior, compared with 56% of Hispanics.

Interestingly, of the 59% of students who say they have sexually harassed someone in the school setting, 94% claim that they themselves have been harassed—98% of girls and 92% of boys.

Just under half (49%) of the student harassers target students of the opposite sex—43% of girls and 54% of boys. One in 10 (11%) admit to having harassed someone of the same sex—this is more common among male harassers (15%)

"I felt distrustful yet good, because somebody noticed something about me."

African American female age 16

■

than female harassers (5%).

Students were provided with a number of reasons why people might engage in harassment and asked which of these reasons applied to their behavior. Of the 37% of perpetrators who say **"It's just part of school life/a lot of people do it/ it's no big deal,"** the gender breakdown is 41% for boys and 31% for girls. Nearly equal percentages of white girls (32%) and African American girls (30%) say this, in contrast with 22% of Hispanic girls. A similar pattern holds true for boys: 41% of whites, 38% of African Americans, and 35% of Hispanics give this reason.

Of the 25% of perpetrators who say that one of the reasons for their behavior is **"I thought the person liked it,"** 27% are boys and 23% are girls, with higher percentages of African Americans claiming this (boys, 38%; girls, 31%).

"**I wanted a date with the person**" is the reason given by 22% of the perpetrators—24% of boys, compared with 20% of girls. "**My friends encouraged me/ 'pushed' me into doing it**" is a reason given by 19%—with no gender gap. "**I wanted something from that person**" is cited by 18% of the perpetrators—20% of boys and 16% of girls. "**I wanted the person to think I had some sort of power over them**" is the response only 6% of perpetrators offered —7% of girls and 6% of boys.

Where is harassment taking place?

The answer is that students, overwhelmingly, are being sexually harassed in hallways and classrooms—school spaces that are generally considered public and safe. Two-thirds (66%) of those who have been harassed say they have been harassed at least once in the **hall**—with girls far more likely to have been targeted there (73%, compared with 58% of boys).

The **classroom** is the second most common sexual harassment site, a distressing finding. More than half (55%) of those who have been harassed say they have been harassed in the classroom— 65% of girls and 44% of boys.

Just over 2 in 5 (43%) say they have been targeted **outside of school, on school grounds** (other than the parking lot)—48% of girls and 39% of boys. Just under 2 in 5 (39%) report that they have been harassed in the **gym**, on the **playing field**, or in the **pool area**, with the gender breakdowns roughly equal. The **cafeteria** is the site reported by one-third (34%) of the

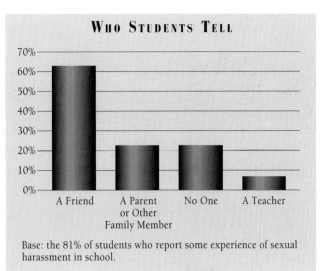

WHO STUDENTS TELL

Base: the 81% of students who report some experience of sexual harassment in school.

"It makes me very angry that these kinds of things can go on in school without being punished..."

Hispanic female age 15

students—again, with no discernible difference between boys and girls, though white boys (37%) are more likely to have been harassed here than African American boys (29%) and Hispanic boys (24%).

Just over 1 in 4 (26%) of students who have been harassed say they have been targeted on **school transportation**— to and from school or on a school trip— with 29% of girls and 22% of boys reporting this. The racial/ethnic gap is notable, with 38% of African American girls citing this, compared with white girls (31%) and Hispanic girls (16%). Just under 1 in 4 students (24%) who have been harassed—evenly split between girls and boys—say they have been harassed at a **field trip** location, with the greatest gaps appearing in the ethnic/racial statistics: African Americans, 28% of girls and 34% of boys; whites, 23% of girls and 22% of boys; Hispanics, 20% of girls and 19% of boys.

Girls—27% (30% for African Americans, 28% for whites, 20% for Hispanics)—are more likely than boys (18%) to have experienced sexual harassment in the **school parking lot**. Conversely, boys (24%) are more likely than girls (14%) to have been harassed in the **locker room**. More significant than the gender gap are the racial/ethnic splits in this category. For girls: 22% for African Americans, 19% for Hispanics, 12% for whites. For boys: 27% of whites report

The statistics in this survey—except where noted—refer to the 81% subgroup of students who report some experience of sexual harassment in school.

this, compared with 19% of Hispanics and 16% of African Americans.

The **boys' rest rooms** are reportedly more dangerous than the **girls' rest rooms**. Of the 10% of harassed students who name these areas, boys outnumber girls 2 to 1 (14% and 7%, respectively).

Who do students tell?

The answer, in broad terms, is that students do not routinely report sexual harassment incidents to adults. In addition, boys who have been harassed are more likely than girls to have told no one (27% and 19%, respectively).

A scant 7% of sexually harassed students say they have told a teacher about the experience, with girls twice as likely as boys to have done this. Just under 1 in 4 (23%) have reported the incidents to parents or other family members—approximately 1 in 3 girls (34%) and 1 in 10 boys (11%), with Hispanic boys (20%) almost twice as likely to respond this way as white and African American boys (11% and 10%, respectively).

By far, most reporting takes place on a peer-to-peer basis: 63% of sexually harassed students have told a friend (49% of boys and 77% of girls).

Those students who have remained silent and told no one number 23%.

> "I wasn't dressed very provocative and I gave them no reason to harass me. I was upset the administration didn't respond immediately after I complained. I was told to ignore the harassers."
>
> White female
> age 16
>
> ■

THE IMPACT

A safe and equitable learning environment is fundamental to academic success. The AAUW Educational Foundation commissioned this survey, the first of its kind, to determine how sexual harassment affects students—educationally, emotionally, and behaviorally.

The findings clearly indicate that although a hostile learning environment has serious implications for both girls and boys, girls report greater problems as a result of sexual harassment, with higher percentages of African American girls reporting this, compared with white and Hispanic girls.

What is the educational impact of sexual harassment?

Nearly 1 in 4 students (23%) who have been sexually harassed say that one outcome of the experience is **not wanting to attend school**: 33% of girls report this—39% of African Americans, compared with 33% of white and 29% of Hispanic girls. In comparison, 12% of boys respond this way: 14% of whites, 9% of African Americans, and 8% of Hispanics. Nearly 1 in 4 girls (24%) say that harassment caused them to **stay home from school or cut a class**.

Nearly 1 in 4 students (23%) report **not wanting to talk as much in class** after experiencing harassment. Once again, the gender gap is considerable, with 32% of girls and 13% of boys thus affected. Almost half the African American girls who have been harassed (42%) respond this way, compared with Hispanic girls (35%) and white girls (30%).

Slightly more than 1 in 5 (21%) students who have been sexually harassed say the

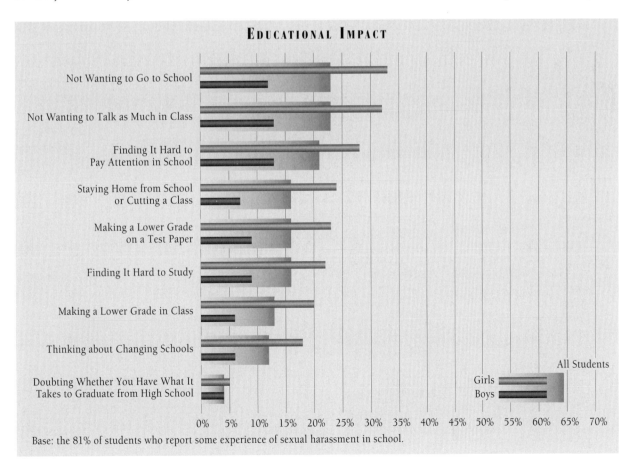

Base: the 81% of students who report some experience of sexual harassment in school.

experience has made it **harder to pay attention in school**, 28% of girls and 13% of boys claim this. Similarly, 16% of students say they have **made a lower grade on a test or paper** as a result of harassment, with 23% of girls and 9% of boys responding in this fashion. Once more, those girls most affected are African American (28%); the numbers are 23% and 22%, respectively, for Hispanics and whites. Of the 13% who say sexual harassment resulted in **making a lower grade in class**, 1 in 5 girls (20%) and 6% of boys report this. African American girls (24%—nearly 1 in 4), again, are most affected, compared with white girls (19%) and Hispanic girls (15%). One in 6 (16%) report that they have **found it hard to study**; 22% of girls answered this way—27% of African Americans, 26% of Hispanics, and 21% of whites.

Thoughts about changing schools are reported by 12% of students who have been

harassed—18% of girls respond this way. Conforming to an unfortunate pattern, African American girls (26%) are more likely to have considered this than white and Hispanic girls (17% each). A small number of students (3%) state that they actually have **changed schools** as a result of sexual harassment.

Finally, 4% say that the experience of sexual harassment has made them **doubt whether they have what it takes to graduate from high school**; 5% of girls say this—almost 1 in 10 (9%) African Americans, 5% of Hispanics, and 4% of whites.

What is the emotional impact of sexual harassment?

While half of all students (50%) who have been harassed state that they have suffered **embarrassment**, nearly 2 in 3 girls (64%) report feeling this way, compared with 36% of boys. White girls and boys feel this in greater numbers than

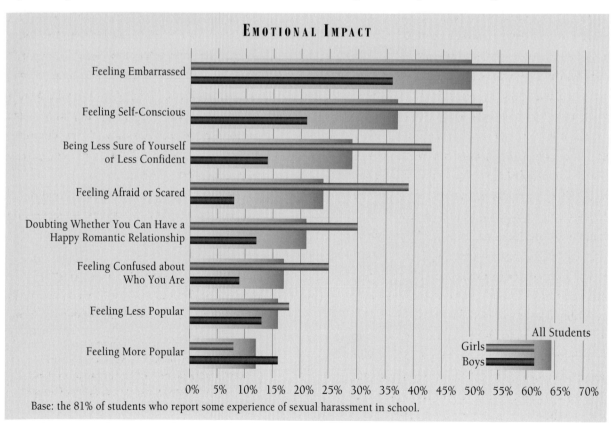

EMOTIONAL IMPACT

Feeling Embarrassed
Feeling Self-Conscious
Being Less Sure of Yourself or Less Confident
Feeling Afraid or Scared
Doubting Whether You Can Have a Happy Romantic Relationship
Feeling Confused about Who You Are
Feeling Less Popular
Feeling More Popular

All Students
Girls
Boys

0% 5% 10% 15% 20% 25% 30% 35% 40% 45% 50% 55% 60% 65% 70%

Base: the 81% of students who report some experience of sexual harassment in school.

their African American and Hispanic counterparts. Racial/ethnic breakdown for girls: whites (66%), Hispanics (58%), African Americans (55%). For boys: whites (40%), African Americans (25%), Hispanics (30%).

Similarly, 37% percent of students say that sexual harassment has caused them to **feel self-conscious**—more than 1 in 2 girls (52%) report this, compared with 1 in 5 boys (21%). Racial/ethnic breakdown for girls: whites (54%), African Americans (47%), Hispanics (44%); for boys: whites (24%), African Americans (14%), Hispanics (22%).

Slightly less than one-third of students (29%) say sexual harassment makes them **feel less sure or less confident about themselves**—43% of girls and 14% of boys say this, a very wide gender gap. Racial/ethnic breakdown for girls: whites (44%), African Americans and Hispanics (38% each); for boys: whites (16%), Hispanics (9%), and African Americans (8%).

When asked if sexual harassment has caused them to **feel afraid or scared**, nearly 1 in 4 (24%) say yes—39% of girls and 8% of boys respond this way, with no marked racial/ethnic gaps. And while slightly more than 1 in 5 sexually harassed students (21%) say that sexual harassment has caused them to **doubt whether they can have a happy romantic relationship**, nearly 1 in 3 girls (30%) report this, compared with 12% of boys. Again, higher percentages of African American girls (38%) respond this way, compared with Hispanic girls (33%) and white girls (27%). For boys, this feeling is more common among Hispanics (16%) and whites (14%). The percentage for African American boys, 8%, is notably smaller compared with the 38% of African American girls who feel this way.

Adolescence is a critical time in the evolution of self-image. In fact, 17% say that sexual harassment has caused them to **feel confused about who they are**. One in 4 girls (25%)

"It made me feel weird. Stupid. Upset."

Hispanic male
age 13

■

react this way; nearly 1 in 3 (31%) Hispanics, 25% of whites, and 21% of African Americans—compared with 1 in 10 boys (9%); 13% of Hispanics, 9% of whites, and 7% of African Americans.

When questioned about their standing among their peers, 16% of students who have been sexually harassed say they **feel less popular** as a result; 18% of girls report this—a striking 21% of whites, compared with 13% of Hispanics and 9% of African Americans. Conversely, 12% of students say the experience of being sexually harassed has caused them to **feel more popular**: twice as many boys (16%) as girls (8%) report this effect. African American girls (16%) are more likely to feel more popular, compared with 7% of white girls and 6% of Hispanic girls. Among boys, the percentages are: African Americans (21%), whites (15%), and Hispanics (14%).

Students were asked which of the following phrases—very upset, somewhat upset, not very upset, not at all upset—best describes how they felt right after being harassed. While 1 in 4 students (25%) report that they were "very upset," 39% of girls—more than 1 in 3—report this, compared with 10% of boys. And **while nearly half the students (48%) say they were "very upset" or "somewhat upset," an alarming 70% of girls respond this way, compared with only 24% of boys**.

Also important to note is that twice as many boys (25%) as girls (13%) say they were not sure how they felt.

What are the behavioral consequences?
Nearly 1 in 2 students (49%) who have been harassed say they **avoid the person(s) who**

The statistics in this survey—except where noted—refer to the 81% subgroup of students who report some experience of sexual harassment in school.

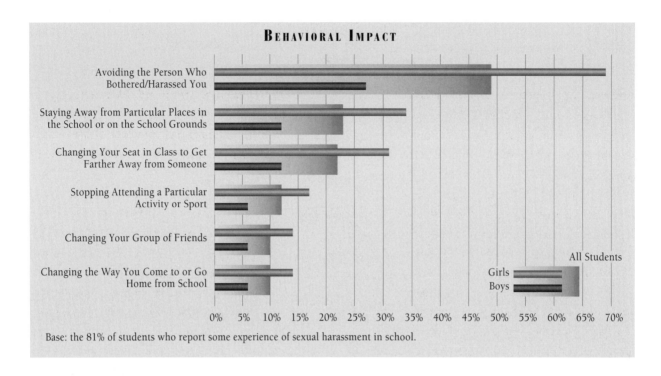

BEHAVIORAL IMPACT

Avoiding the Person Who Bothered/Harassed You

Staying Away from Particular Places in the School or on the School Grounds

Changing Your Seat in Class to Get Farther Away from Someone

Stopping Attending a Particular Activity or Sport

Changing Your Group of Friends

Changing the Way You Come to or Go Home from School

All Students
Girls
Boys

0% 5% 10% 15% 20% 25% 30% 35% 40% 45% 50% 55% 60% 65% 70%

Base: the 81% of students who report some experience of sexual harassment in school.

harassed them; a whopping 69% of girls, compared with 27% of boys, report responding this way. Slightly less than 1 in 4 students (23%) say they **stay away from particular places in the school or on the school grounds**; 34% of girls report this—41% of African Americans, 37% of Hispanics, and 32% of whites—compared with 12% of boys.

Further, nearly 1 in 4 students (22%) say that sexual harassment has at least on one occasion caused them to **change their seats in class**; 31% of girls respond this way—42% of African American girls, 30% of white girls, and 28% of Hispanic girls—compared with 12% of boys. More than 1 in 10 (12%) have **stopped attend-**

"It made me feel that a woman isn't worth much, and it shouldn't be that way."

White female age 16

ing a particular activity or sport; 17% of girls (nearly 1 out of 5) react this way—27% of Hispanics, 22% of African Americans, and 16% of whites—compared with 6% of boys.

One in 10 students (10%) report **changing their group of friends**—14% of girls and 6% of boys respond in this fashion. The numbers are the same for the incidence of those who **changed the way they come to or go home from school** (10% of students; 14% of girls and 6% of boys), although in this category there is a notable racial/ethnic gap: 25% of African American girls react this way, compared with 20% of Hispanic girls and 12% of white girls.

THE STEREOTYPE

Despite the stereotype of males as harassers, significant numbers of boys (76%) report being targets of sexual harassment in school. The numbers are particularly high for African American boys, most notably in the categories involving direct physical contact. Hispanic boys, on the other hand, are the least likely to experience nonphysical forms of sexual harassment. In addition, boys are most often harassed by a girl acting alone.

The most common form of harassment experienced by boys involves being the target of **sexual comments, jokes, gestures, or looks**—more than half those boys surveyed (56%) have been thus targeted, compared with 76% of girls.

Two in five boys (42%) have experienced being **touched, grabbed, or pinched in a sexual way**, compared with 65% of girls. Among those boys who have been **intentionally brushed up against in a sexual way** (36%), African Americans (49%) have been targeted most, compared with whites (34%) and Hispanics (29%). In the case of those who have been **flashed or mooned**, the gender gap narrows: 41% of boys and 49% of girls have been the target of this conduct. Similarly, roughly equal numbers of boys and girls say they have been **shown, given, or left sexual pictures, photographs, illustrations, messages, or notes**: 31% of boys and 34% of girls.

Among boys, 34% have been the **target of sexual rumors**, compared with 42% of girls.

African American boys (38%) have experienced having their **clothes pulled at in a sexual way** in greater numbers than Hispanic and white boys (25% for each group).

The gender breakdown is very close in the instances of **clothing being pulled off or down**:

"Makes me

feel kind of

alone

because if

my brothers

were with

me they

wouldn't let

it go on."

African American
male
age 13

17% of boys and 16% of girls have been targeted in this way. Again, among boys African Americans have the highest numbers: nearly 1 in 4 (23%) report having experienced this type of harassment.

In addition, twice as many boys (23%) as girls (10%) have been **called gay**.

Very troubling is the 9% of boys who say they have been **forced to do something sexual at school other than kissing**: 1 in 5 African American boys (19%) have been targeted this way, compared with 13% of Hispanic boys and 6% of white boys.

In terms of **who is doing the harassing**, 57% of boys who have been harassed report having been targeted by a female acting alone, 35% by a group of females, 25% by a male acting alone, 14% by a group of males, 13% by a mixed group of females and males.

Regarding **sites of harassment**, boys who have been harassed (24%) are more likely than girls (14%) to have been targeted in the locker room and twice as likely to have been harassed in the rest room (14% for boys and 7% for girls).

Boys are more likely than girls to tell no one they have been sexually harassed (27% and 19%, respectively).

Boys who have been harassed say that as a result they: feel embarrassed (36%), are not sure how they feel (25%), feel self-conscious (21%), feel more popular (16%), feel less sure of themselves or less confident (14%), do not talk as much in class (13%), find it hard to pay attention in class (13%), don't want to go to school (12%), doubt they can have a happy romantic relationship (12%). Again these numbers are smaller than those for their female counterparts in every category.

The Worst Harassment— Being Called Gay

Sexual identity is a sensitive issue for adolescents. During this time, being called gay or lesbian is disturbing to a majority of students. Indeed, when students were asked to what degree they would be upset if they were the targets of the 14 different types of sexual harassment outlined in the survey, 86% of all students surveyed said they would be "very upset" if they were called gay or lesbian: 85% of boys and 87% of girls. No other type of harassment—including actual physical abuse—provoked a reaction this strong among boys.

In terms of actual experience, 17% of students say they have been called gay or lesbian. Boys (23%) are more than twice as likely as girls (10%) to have been targeted this way, with no significant racial/ethnic variations. Among the boys, 4% say this has occurred often; 5%, occasionally; 14%, rarely. Twice as many Hispanic boys (8%) say they are often called gay, compared with 4% each for African American and white boys.

Of those boys who have been called gay, nearly 3 in 5 (58%) say they have called someone else gay: 61% of whites, 51% of African Americans, and 45% of Hispanics.

> "Made me feel great that someone likes me...except for fags— I would hate that."
>
> White male age 15
>
> ■

The statistics in this survey—except where noted—refer to the 81% subgroup of students who report some experience of sexual harassment in school.

THE CHALLENGE

This survey, comprised of voices as well as numbers, shapes a picture that demands attention: sexual harassment in school—in hallways, classrooms, and beyond—is widespread, with both girls and boys being targeted by their peers as well as adults. Clearly, the process of getting an education is a large enough challenge for most students without the added challenge of contending with sexual harassment in school.

At the most basic, schools must have sexual harassment policies that are clearly communicated and routinely enforced. The mere fact that more than half the students surveyed (57%) do not know if their school has a policy on sexual harassment is disturbing.

As with past AAUW Educational Foundation research, we are confident that the results of this survey will become a focal point on the agendas of policy makers, educators, and others concerned with the education of America's children. Indeed, there is more work to be done, and the Foundation will continue to fund research, community action projects, and teachers. And the American Association of University Women, with more than 130,000 members nationwide, will continue its work in coalition with

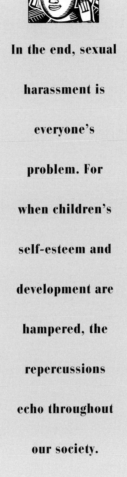

In the end, sexual harassment is everyone's problem. For when children's self-esteem and development are hampered, the repercussions echo throughout our society.

other groups and individuals to help ensure that the educational experiences of all public school students are positive and life-enriching.

While this survey establishes that sexual harassment in school is widespread, it also raises some important questions. Does adult sexual harassment have roots in school-based behavior? When behavior is shrugged off as permissible because it is widespread and "boys will be boys," are we unwittingly setting the stage for abusive behavior later on? Do students harass because they themselves are harassed?

The statements and statistics presented here add up to an undeniable mandate: parents, teachers, and administrators must acknowledge that sexual harassment in school is creating a hostile environment that compromises the education of America's children. Sexual harassment is clearly and measurably taking a toll on a significant percentage of students' educational, emotional, and behavioral lives. And although girls are experiencing more harassment—and suffering graver consequences—in the end, sexual harassment is everyone's problem. For when children's self-esteem and development are hampered, the repercussions echo throughout our society.

Sexual harassment in school is wide-spread.

- Four in 5 students (81%) say they have experienced some form of sexual harassment during their school lives: 85% of girls and 76% of boys.

- One in 4 students (25%) have experienced 1 or more of the 14 surveyed types of sexual harassment in school and say they are targeted "often."

- More than half the students surveyed (58%) report that they have been targeted "often" or "occasionally."

There are notable gender and racial/ethnic gaps.

- Nearly 1 in 3 girls (31%) who have been harassed have experienced unwanted advances "often," compared with fewer than 1 in 5 boys (18%).

- Two in 3 girls (66%) who have been harassed report that they have been targeted "often" or "occasionally." This is true for fewer than 1 in 2 boys (49%).

- For girls, 87% of whites report having experienced sexual harassment, compared with 84% of African Americans and 82% of Hispanics

- Among boys, African Americans (81%) have experienced sexual harassment, compared with whites (75%) and Hispanics (69%).

In grades 7, 8, and 9, many more girls than boys first experience sexual harassment in school.

- One in 3 students (32%) who have been harassed* first experience sexual harassment in grade 6 or earlier.

"The

experience

was

unnerving.

I was rattled.

I felt

insecure and

vulnerable at

school,

which should

be a safe

place for

learning."

African American
female
age 18

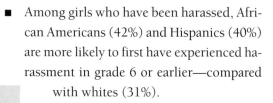

- Among girls who have been harassed, African Americans (42%) and Hispanics (40%) are more likely to first have experienced harassment in grade 6 or earlier—compared with whites (31%).

- For 6% of students who have been harassed, the first experience of sexual harassment took place before grade 3.

- Twice as many boys (36%) as girls (18%) are unable to recall the grade in which they were first harassed in school.

Sexual comments, jokes, looks, and gestures—as well as touching, grabbing, and/or pinching in a sexual way—are commonplace in school.

- Two in 3 of all students surveyed (66%) have been targets of the above forms of verbal/gestural abuse.

- 65% of all girls and 42% of all boys surveyed have experienced touching, grabbing, and/or pinching in a sexual way.

The third most common form of sexual harassment in school involves intentionally brushing up against someone in a sexual way—something girls experience far more often than boys.

- 57% of all girls surveyed have experienced this, in contrast to 36% of boys.

- Among all girls surveyed, African Americans (64%) have been the target of this physical form of harassment,

*The statistics in this survey—except where noted—refer to the 81% subgroup of students who report some experience of sexual harassment in school.

compared with whites (58%) and Hispanics (49%).

- Among all boys surveyed, nearly half of African Americans (49%) experienced this behavior, compared with a third or less of whites (34%) and Hispanics (29%).

Students say they would be very upset if they were called gay or lesbian. Being called gay would be more upsetting to boys than actual physical abuse.

- 86% of all students say they would be very upset if they were called gay or lesbian—85% of boys and 87% of girls respond this way.

- For boys, this is the most disturbing form of unwanted behavior: 88% of Hispanic boys and 85% of both African American and white boys would be troubled by being called gay.

- 17% of students say they have been called lesbian or gay when they didn't want to be—10% of girls and 23% of boys.

- Of those boys who have been called gay, more than half (58%) say they have called someone else gay.

"I felt like a slut. I never wanted him to do this, but he did. I felt gross."

Hispanic female
age 14

- Two in 3 (66%) of all boys and more than half (52%) of all girls say they have sexually harassed someone in the school setting.

- Similarly, of the 59% of students who admit to having perpetrated sexual harassment in school, 94% say they, themselves, have been harassed—98% of girl harassers and 92% of boy harassers.

  - Among all girls surveyed: African Americans (63%) are more likely to have harassed than Hispanics and whites (50% for each group).

  - Among all boys surveyed, roughly equal percentages of African Americans (67%) and whites (66%), compared with 56% of Hispanics, admit to having perpetrated such behavior.

  - Half of those students (49%) who have harassed someone at school admit to having harassed a student of the opposite sex—43% of girls and 54% of boys say this. More than 1 in 10 (11%) admit to having harassed someone of the same sex as themselves—15% of boys and 5% of girls.

Experiences of student-to-student harassment outnumber all others, with notable gender and ethnic/racial gaps.

- Nearly 4 in 5 students (79%) who have been harassed have been targeted by peers: current or former students.

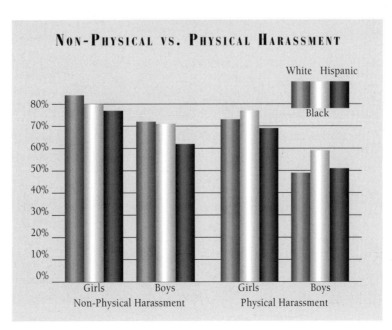

NON-PHYSICAL VS. PHYSICAL HARASSMENT

White   Hispanic
Black

Girls   Boys
Non-Physical Harassment

Girls   Boys
Physical Harassment

- Among girls who have been harassed: 81% report having been harassed by a male acting alone, 57% by a group of males.

- Among boys who have been harassed: 57% report having been harassed by a female acting alone.

Adult-to-student harassment is nonetheless considerable, with notable gender and ethnic/racial gaps.

- 18% of students who have been harassed cite adults as the perpetrators.

- One in 4 girls (25%) and 1 in 10 boys (10%) who have been harassed say they have been harassed by a school employee (such as a teacher, coach, bus driver, teacher's aide, security guard, principal, or counselor).

- Among girls, adult-student harassment is more commonly experienced by African Americans (33%) than whites (25%) and Hispanics (17%).

Harassing others is a routine part of school culture—more so for boys than for girls.

- Of those students who admit to having sexually harassed someone, 37% say "It's just part of school life/a lot of people do it/it's no big deal"—41% of boys and 31% of girls.

- Of the 25% of perpetrators who say "I thought the person liked it," 27% are boys and 23% are girls.

Public areas are the most common harassment sites—especially as reported by girls.

- Two in 3 students who have been harassed (66%) say they have been harassed in the hallway.

- More than half (55%) of those who have been harassed cite the classroom.

- Far more girls than boys have been harassed in the hallway (73% and 58%, respectively). The same holds true for the classroom: 65% of girls and 44% of boys report being harassed here.

- More than 2 in 5 harassed students (43%) have been targeted outside of school, on

> "I don't care. People do this stuff every day. No one feels insulted by it. That's stupid. We just play around. I think sexual harassment is normal."
>
> White male age 14

school grounds (other than the parking lot).

- More than one-third of students have been harassed in the school cafeteria, most notably white boys (37%), compared with African American boys (29%) and Hispanic boys (24%).

- More than 1 in 4 students (26%) have been harassed on school transportation (to and from school; on school trips). 38% of African American girls cite this, compared with 31% of white girls and 16% of Hispanic girls.

Students usually do not report incidents to adults. Boys are more likely than girls to tell no one.

- Fewer than 1 in 10 students who have been harassed (7%) say they have told a teacher, although girls are twice as likely to have done so as boys.

- Fewer than 1 in 4 students who have been harassed (23%) say they told a parent or other family member— roughly 1 in 3 girls (34%) and 1 in 10 boys (11%).

- 63% of harassed students say they told a friend—77% of girls and 49% of boys.

- 23% of harassed students say they told no one—27% of boys and 19% of girls.

Notably higher numbers of girls than boys say they have suffered as a result of sexual harassment in school; African American girls have suffered the most.

- Nearly 1 in 4 students (23%) who have been sexually harassed say that as a result they did not want to attend school: 33% of girls, compared with 12% of boys. The numbers are very similar for those who say they do not want to talk as much in class after having experienced harassment.

- Among harassed girls: 39% of African Americans did not want to attend school, in contrast with 33% of whites and 29% of Hispanics. Among harassed boys, the numbers are: 14% of whites, 9% of African Americans, and 8% of Hispanics.

- While half of all students who have been harassed (50%) state they have suffered embarrassment, nearly 2 in 3 girls (64%) report feeling this way, compared with roughly 1 in 3 (36%) boys.

- 37% of harassed students say that sexual harassment has caused them to feel self-conscious—1 in 2 girls (52%), compared with 1 in 5 boys (21%).

- Slightly less than one-third of harassed students (29%) report feeling less sure or less confident about themselves—43% of girls, compared with 14% of boys.

- Nearly half the students (48%) who were harassed say they were "very upset" or "somewhat upset" after having been harassed—an alarming 70% of girls respond this way. Twice as many boys (25%) as girls (13%) say they were not sure how they felt.

- One in 4 students (24%) of those harassed say the experience left them feeling afraid or scared—39% of girls and 8% of boys.

- Slightly more than 1 in 5 students who have been harassed (21%) say that harassment caused them to doubt whether they can have a happy romantic relationship—30% of girls, compared with 12% of boys. Higher percentages of African American girls respond this way (38%), compared with Hispanic girls (33%) and white girls (27%).

- Nearly 1 in 2 harassed students (49%) say they avoid the person(s) who harassed them, with 69% of girls responding this way.

> **"It made me feel low. Thought that I was dirt. I just wanted to die."**
>
> African American female age 14

- Slightly less than 1 in 4 students (23%) who have been harassed say they stay away from particular places in the school or outside on school grounds. 34% of girls report this—41% of African Americans, compared with 37% of Hispanics and 32% of whites.

Boys routinely experience harassment. Among African Americans, the incidence of harassment involving direct physical contact is alarming.

- 57% of boys who have been harassed have been targeted by a girl, 35% by a group of girls.

- 25% of boys who have been harassed have been targeted by another boy, 14% by a group of boys.

- 10% of harassed boys have been targeted by a teacher or other school employee.

- 24% of harassed boys, compared with 14% of harassed girls, have been targeted in the locker room.

- Boys who have been harassed (14%) are twice as likely as girls who have been harassed (7%) to be targeted in the rest room.

- Half of all African American boys surveyed (49%) have been intentionally brushed up against in a sexual way.

- One in 5 African American boys surveyed (22%) have been forced to kiss someone; 19% have been forced to do something sexual other than kissing.

The statistics in this survey—except where noted—refer to the 81% subgroup of students who report some experience of sexual harassment in school.

Resources: The AAUW Equity Library

Ground-breaking Works on Gender Bias in Education

Hostile Hallways: The AAUW Survey on Sexual Harassment in America's Schools
The first national study of sexual harassment, based on the experiences of 1,632 students in grades 8 through 11. Gender and ethnic/racial (African American, Hispanic, and white) data breakdowns included. Commissioned by the AAUW Educational Foundation and conducted by Louis Harris and Associates. 28 pages/1993. $8.95 AAUW members/$11.95 nonmembers.

The AAUW Report: How Schools Shortchange Girls
Disturbing report documents girls' second-class treatment in America's schools, grades K–12. The research report, prepared by the Wellesley College Center for Research on Women, includes policy recommendations and strategies for change. 128 pages/1992. $14.95 AAUW members/$16.95 nonmembers.

The AAUW Report Executive Summary
Overview of **The AAUW Report** research, with recommendations for educators and policymakers. 8 pages/1992. $6.95 AAUW members/$8.95 nonmembers.

The AAUW Report Action Guide
Strategies for combating gender bias in school, based on **The AAUW Report** recommendations. 8 pages/1992. $6.95 AAUW members/$8.95 nonmembers.

AAUW Issue Briefs
Package of five briefs, with strategies for change: Equitable Treatment of Girls and Boys in the Classroom; Restructuring Education; Stalled Agenda—Gender Equity and the Training of Educators; College Admission Tests: Opportunities or Roadblocks?; Creating a Gender-Fair Multicultural Curriculum. 1990-93. $7.95 AAUW members/$9.95 nonmembers.

Shortchanging Girls, Shortchanging America
Highly readable executive summary of the 1991 poll that awakened the nation to the problem of gender bias in America's schools. Poll shows graphically how classroom gender bias hurts girls' self-esteem, school achievement, and career aspirations. Revised edition, with updated account of poll's impact and review of school, community, and government action strategies, highlights survey results with charts and graphs. 20 pages/1994. $8.95 AAUW members/$11.95 nonmembers.

Full Data Report: Shortchanging Girls, Shortchanging America
Complete data on AAUW's 1991 national poll on girls and self-esteem, with survey questions and responses, and banners displaying cross-tabulations. Includes floppy disk with all data. 500 pages/1991. *To order, call 202/785-7761.*

Video: Shortchanging Girls, Shortchanging America
A dramatic look at the inequities girls face in school. Features education experts and public policy leaders, AAUW poll results, as well as the compelling voices and faces of American girls. VHS format/15 minutes/1991. $19.95 AAUW members/$24.95 nonmembers.

Action Alert
Monthly newsletter published by the AAUW Program and Policy Department monitors congressional action on educational equity as well as reproductive choice, sexual harassment, and other vital issues. Gives you the information you need to lobby effectively for change. One-year subscription: $20 AAUW members/$25 nonmembers.

Help Make a Difference for Today's Girls...and Tomorrow's Leaders.

Hostile Hallways: The AAUW Survey on Sexual Harassment in America's Schools is made possible by charitable contributions to the AAUW Educational Foundation, a not-for-profit 501(c)(3) organization. Help us continue breaking ground toward positive societal changes. Your support can help put an end to sexual harassment and inequity in schools and communities throughout the nation. Your contributions make a difference, supporting research, community action projects, fellowships for women, and teachers. Send your contributions to: AAUW Educational Foundation, Dept. T, 1111 Sixteenth Street N.W., Washington, DC 20036-4873.

Become part of the American Association of University Women, representing 150,000 college graduates, and help promote education and equity for women and girls. You can add your voice as a Member-at-Large or work on critical issues in one of AAUW's 1,750 local branches. For further membership information, write: AAUW Membership, Dept. T, 1111 Sixteenth Street N.W., Washington, DC 20036-4873.

AAUW Resources Order Form

Name _____

Address _____

City/State/Zip _____

Daytime phone _____ AAUW membership # (if applicable) _____

Item	Circle Price Member/Nonmember	Quantity	Total
Hostile Hallways	$8.95/$11.95	_____	_____
The AAUW Report	$14.95/$16.95	_____	_____
AAUW Report Summary	$6.95/$8.95	_____	_____
AAUW Report Action Guide	$6.95/$8.95	_____	_____
Issue Briefs 5-Pack	$7.95/$9.95	_____	_____
Shortchanging Girls: Summary	$8.95/$11.95	_____	_____
Shortchanging Girls: Video	$19.95/$24.95	_____	_____
Action Alert	$20/$25 per year	_____	_____
		Subtotal:	_____
		6% sales tax (DC, FL residents only)	_____
		Shipping/Handling:	$4.00
AAUW Membership	$35	_____	_____
		Total Order:	_____

For *bulk pricing on orders of 10 or more*, call 800/225-9998, ext. 246.

Please make check or money order payable to AAUW. Do not send cash.

Credit cards are accepted for orders of $10 or more.

☐ MasterCard ☐ Visa Card #__ __ __ __ - __ __ __ __ - __ __ __ __ - __ __ __ __ Expiration _____

Name on card _____ Cardholder signature _____

SATISFACTION GUARANTEED: If you are not completely satisfied with your purchase, please return it within 90 days for exchange, credit, or refund. Videos are returnable only if defective, and for replacement only.

☐ Please send me information on joining an AAUW branch in my area (dues vary by branch).

☐ I'd like to join as a Member-at-Large. Enclosed is $35. (Fill in education information below.)

_____

College/University   State/Campus   Year/Degree

FOR MAIL ORDERS, SEND THIS FORM TO:
AAUW Sales Office
Dept. 246
P.O. Box 251
Annapolis Junction, MD 20701-0251

FOR TELEPHONE ORDERS, CALL:
800/225-9998, ext. 246

CODE: D95ROS

X